Seeing Sounds

Xavier Pastrano

Copyright © Xavier Pastrano

Cover photo by Alex Gutzmer
Edited by Janet Pischke
All rights reserved. No part of this book may be used or reproduced in any manner without written permission from the author except in the case of brief quotations included in articles and reviews.

Harsan Publishing

www.harsanpublishing.com
www.xppoetry.com

To those who believe in the power of music and words.

Table of Contents

Theme of Rome..................................6

Freedom Blade..................................8

There are Many of Us..................................10

Arco Arena..................................12

Christmas Time is Here..................................14

Landing Cliffs..................................16

Trouble..................................18

Bats in Attic..................................20

St. Ides Heaven..................................22

Maw..................................24

Beyond..................................26

Broken Ground..................................28

Summit Reprise..................................30

Twinkler..................................32

Ethel..................................34

Seeing Sounds

Theme of "Rome"

Ungluing themselves from each other,
my eyelids open slowly like
the doors of crypts
kept closed for decades.

Synapses connect,
sending signals to extremities,
reanimating a minimalism of mobility.

Once upright,
after invoking the prowess of Lazarus,
my sluggish procession then begins:
El andar de los muertos.

A daily ritual,
a great pilgrimage through
a dimly lit living room to
the exquisite glass carafe.

It holds exotic elixirs from
Ethiopia,
to Guatemala,
to Costa Rica…
a distillate
imbibed
to help me concentrate,
summoning the strength needed
to aid in my functioning
as a semi-conscious human being.

Pastrano

Seeing Sounds

Freedom Blade

Gray waves
rise and fall like my chest.
They carry an energy
(that originated on another shore)
across a great expanse
to the here and now,
where it rocks me to sleep with its lullaby
while I lay in the sand.
Mist
descends from the sky,
kisses my lips and stipples
the surface of the ocean.
Pregnant drops
make contact, casting
ripples that
echo for eons,
reaching beyond boundaries our eyes can see,
and drifting
to places that can only be felt.

Pastrano

An excerpt from the journal I kept during my wife's pregnancy

10:05 PM - 12/15/14: Hi, Sweet Pea! Last night, your mom and I wanted to do something special with you, so we got out my iPod and her headphones. Last night, you listened to your very first song... Music has played a powerful and positive role in our lives... We chose the song "Freedom Blade" by a band called This Will Destroy You. Although the name sounds intense, this particular song is quite serene and beautiful. It was the song that brought your mom and I together when I was in Norway and she was in Sioux Falls. We also used the song in our wedding. To us, the song represents our love for one another and our story. And since you are now an amazing part of our lives, we wanted to share it with you because we love you so very very much.

All my love,

Dad

Seeing Sounds

There are Many of Us

My child,
we live in a world of dirt
in which we wriggle,
searching for sustenance and safety.

We live under a sun
that can scorch and warm,
under a sky
that can flood and nourish.

As you make your way through the dirt,
you'll grow,
and witness the splendor that can bud
when elements work in tandem:
when sun, soil, and rain
produce an abundance of fertile thoughts,
forged to yield a fruitful future.

However,
despite my greatest efforts,
you'll also experience
discordant winds of change
that'll howl and uproot
all that is good.

You'll get burned by an unforgiving sun,
drowned by rains of sorrow
and experience hurt
that will scar and stymie,
but such is the way
when growing in a world of dirt;

Remember
that soil can salve
the most savage wounds,
Return to it,
as need be,
and let it enfold you,
for it will foster strength
and resilience.
It will reinforce your roots
to withstand the most brutal winds
and dire conditions.
It will make you shine.

Pastrano

Seeing Sounds

Arco Arena

The pasque flowers bow in adoration of the South
as the North winds whistle and whip around
purple petals.

Prairie grass susurrates
and dry stems mimic
the chirping of crickets
all while the moon hails
the Coyote Queen.

She sings,
in shadows,
the rites
native to her tongue,
concluding the evening's ritual
with the echoes of her howls:
filling the canyons
with her power and pride.

Pastrano

Seeing Sounds

Christmas Time is Here

Hues
of blue and green
cocoon
an amorphous moon,
moving in slo-mo.
It loses its shape
then finds a new one,
rotating,
in a gyrating, hula hooping swoop.
Cilia pitter patter
in alternating oscillations:
resembling
perpetual peaks and valleys
in rhythmic wavelengths.

Pastrano

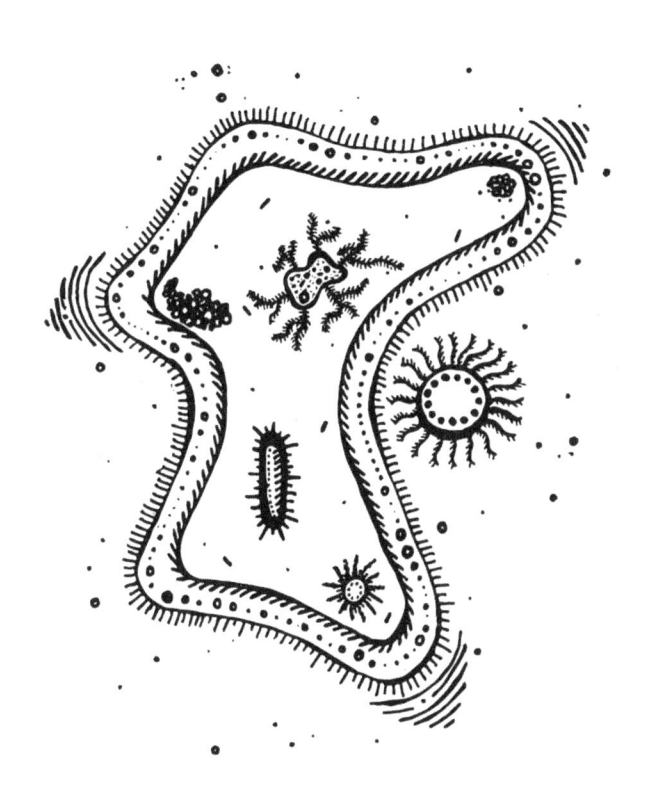

Seeing Sounds

Landing Cliffs

I can feel my heart
beat beating in my head
as I close my eyes and sink
through my chair.

The bourbon is working.

Hushed guitar tones and
kick snare metronomes spin
at 33 and ⅓.

See,
I've finally returned to a peace of mind
taken away from me by
A-N-X-I-E-T-Why?

While Landing Cliffs spins
I'm reunited
with the part of me
not covered in tar,
unscathed and unmarred,
the part rooted in peace,
so I reach out to grab it
and take it back with me,
to have and hold
before the needle lifts.

Pastrano

Seeing Sounds

Trouble

Despite my battle jacket
covered in pins and patches that peg
me as
a metalhead &
a misanthrope &
a pursuer of doom inducing riffs
by bands whose names are plays
on Tolkien characters and bongs,
you're the song
with the most plays in my library:
130
an unseen emblem,
stitched to the inside of my chest,
that speaks louder
than the ones that adorn
my denim coat.

Pastrano

Seeing Sounds

Bats in the Attic

The image outside his
picture window
was like a scene from a movie.
Snowflakes were floating in
slo-mo, sideways trajectories, like
miniature meteorites
flying down from the heavens
and crash landing in heaps upon the earth.

Behind the veil of scuttling flurries,
behind framed panes of glass,
he watched,
from the comfort of his favorite chair,
cars, vans, and trucks
whirr along the interstate
in uncanny silence:
observing in astonishment
the daily goings-on
of those willing to brave the world.

And just when he thought
he had had enough of feeling lonely
and felt like he could maybe do it,
that he could maybe join them out there,

just as his sweaty palms
pressed into the fabric of the armrests
of his familiar chair,
pushing himself up
with the intention
to go out into the world
that he had removed himself from,

he heard his neighbors
enter their apartment next door,
heard their muffled dialogue,
sounding like ghosts of previous tenants
trapped in the walls,
continuing unfinished conversations
from the past.

His muscles relaxed
and his weight settled back into the chair.

And with feelings
of repose and chagrin,
he thought to himself,
with assurance,
"The ghosts will keep me company today."

Pastrano

Seeing Sounds

St. Ides Heaven

We slid into each other's arms so easily,
like a pair of broken in Chucks.
Busted, split, seemingly worthless to others,
we cast a strange magic on one another,
imposing importance
and nostalgia
in the other's eyes.

Yet,
despite the comfort
and familiarity,
the countless walks
over the same cracked pavements,
we wore each other thin and threadless,
until our soles became haggard
and flapped like loose lips,
insoles exposed, slapping with each kick
and step.

In discordant beats,
we stepped on each other's laces
out of spite,
trying to redress and redirect.

A push-me-pull-you in full effect
causing us to trip and fall
into the street,
then smoked by a car
and stripped from the feet
 that kept us together.

With busted eyelets
and our tongues hanging out,
we were beyond repair.

We occupied the curbs
and people wondered how we got there,
and without looking up we'd casually say,
"It was someone I loved."

So now we wait
to see if one of us gets upcycled
or kicked along the curb.
Either way,
we were destined for self-destruction.

Pastrano

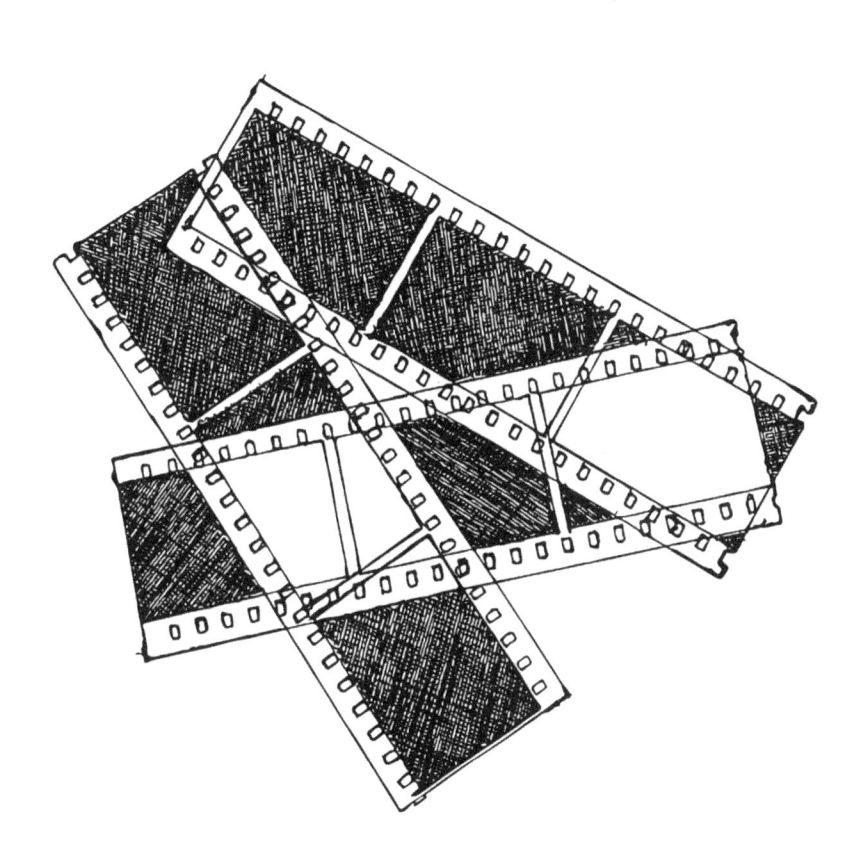

Seeing Sounds

Maw

When I laid my head upon my pillow,
sleep opened its maw.

Rolling out its crimson tongue like
a budded red carpet,
it invited me in and
enfolded me with balmy breath,
slowly closing
its gaping hole behind me.

Shrouded in darkness,
my only company
was the thud of its heartbeat,
a reverberating reverie,
pounding my ear drums and
playing my temples like timpanies
with each pulsating thrum
thrust through the corridors of its throat.

I walked forward aimlessly
along obsidian walls that
contracted,
reacted to my touch
as I blindly slid my hands
over ribbed passageways, damp
with sputum.

My sputtered breathing echoed
through the black,
and came back to me
in waves of mockery,
as a chorus chanting,

"You are mine.
You will stay.
You will venerate.
I will prey."

I
am Jonah.

But in this existence,
there is no god.

There is only me,
the beast,
and the darkness of everlasting
sleep.

Pastrano

Seeing Sounds

Beyond

I saw your finger
tapping to the beat of my heart
because you could hear it
from across the rope bridge.

It sounded hollow in my head,
yet,
the drone rattled my guts
and blurred my vision.
But we stood
staring
like two gunslingers,
waiting to draw,
shooting to kill.

I watched you whisper incantations.
Watched them
slither across the chasm,
felt them,
enter my nostrils
and slide down the back of my throat.
They tasted of loam,
and charcoal.

I fell to my knees,
and you opened your mouth.
The coals
you had swallowed
caused your throat to glow,
and in a whispering breath,
the bridge caught flame.

In that moment,
my final, fiery descent,
I saw what it meant to be you.

Pastrano

Broken Ground

Surrounded by a dying world,
I prodded the dying embers of my fire
and watched them cast crude silhouettes
on the cave walls,
watched
the shadows dance
and reenact the fall.

We were naive:
not blind,
but unwilling to see that
Pestilence, War, Famine, and Death
would not be sent by a god
nor arrive on black clouds
in a reverie of horns,
but rather
hissed in syllables
and writhing in words,
spoken
by gilded tongues in suits that promised
coveted fruits.

Denial was sweet,
so we
suckled the saccharine nectar
from Lady Liberty's infected teat.
We consumed the lot,
and laughed
as minds and teeth fell to rot,
because it was then that we realized,
as bellies busted
from candied chicanery,
that we
were our own worst enemies:
the guilty culprits
of our omnicidal trajectory.

Pastrano

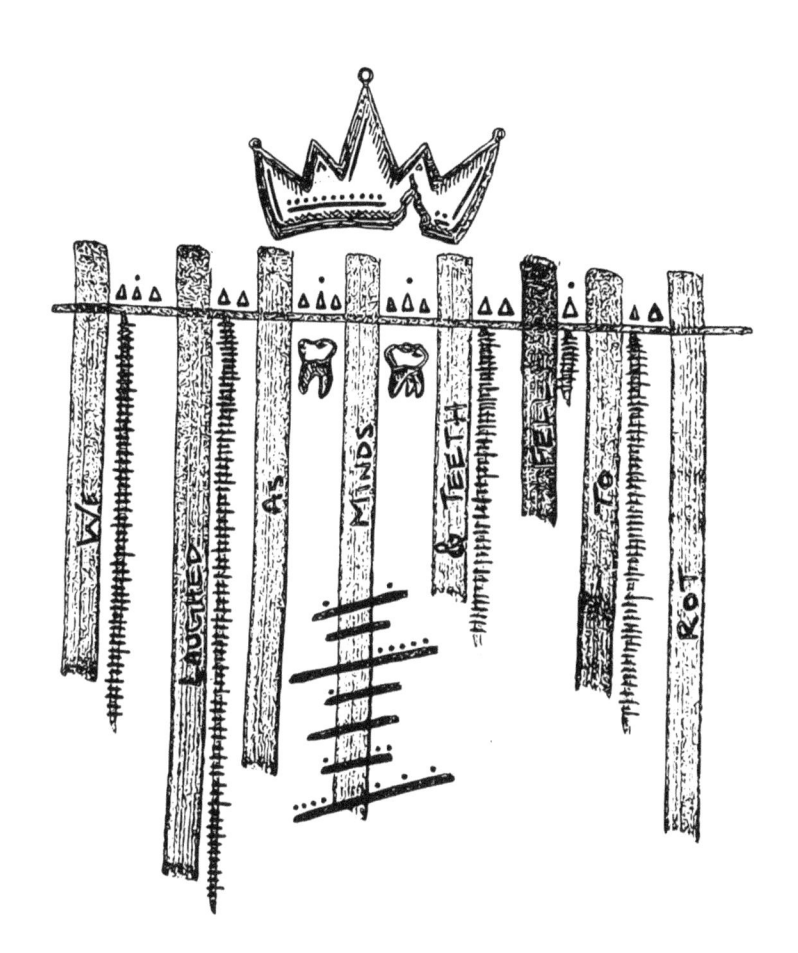

Summit Reprise

While lost and drowning in a morphine sea,
I fought to lift my lids and set my eyes
on that which had come forth to visit me.

It did not bother to come forth in guise:
arriving in a plume of acrid smoke
and bellowing a dirge of trumpet cries.

Twas' shrouded in an iridescent cloak
and riding on a wave of bitter fog,
it levitated over me and spoke.

Its breath was damp and smelled of rot and bog
and then I understood it all too well;
"this visitor will scribe my epilogue,

then groan the incantations of a spell,
and skin me of this fleshy, mortal shell."

Pastrano

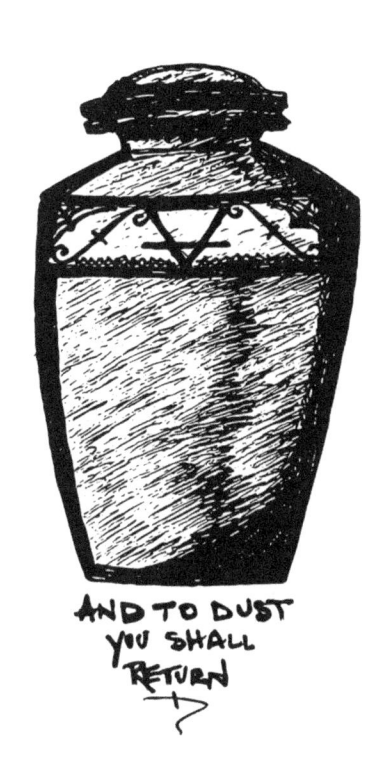

Seeing Sounds

Twinkler

When the cremator slowly roared to life,
your collective sobs sounded
like a swarm of bees,
muffled from the heat
and the furnace's heartbeat.

The mortician pushed the button
and I was rolled into the retort;
ushered under archways of refractory bricks
that hummed hymns of conservation,
of change
from one phase to another.

And when the fire took what was left
and turned it into a harlequin ash,
I moved past the threshold
and transcended,
becoming the gravity
that pulled your tears down your cheeks
and the static zap
that you felt
when you embraced our son.

Pastrano

Seeing Sounds

Ethel

I wish you could see the sun right now.
Rising slowly, stubbornly,
like an ancient colossus
forced to awaken from a century of sleep,
shuddering loose from the horizon.

The accumulated dust of yesterday
shifts
from vibrations
as the behemoth star groans to life
and begins its ascension.

Our hopes, fears, decisions, actions
of the previous day
are disturbed
from their provisional resting place,
and fall in a cascade
of showering memories,
wiped away like sleep
from the eye of a giant.

As it climbs higher
into the firmament,
and finally peeks over the divide,
its light hits the ground
running
and plows forward
like
an incandescent comber,
swelling
as its rays consume inch after inch
of gelid ground,
running
from a previous life,
racing
towards a new day,
burning
our shadows onto the walls
to show us who we were
and where we've been.

Pastrano

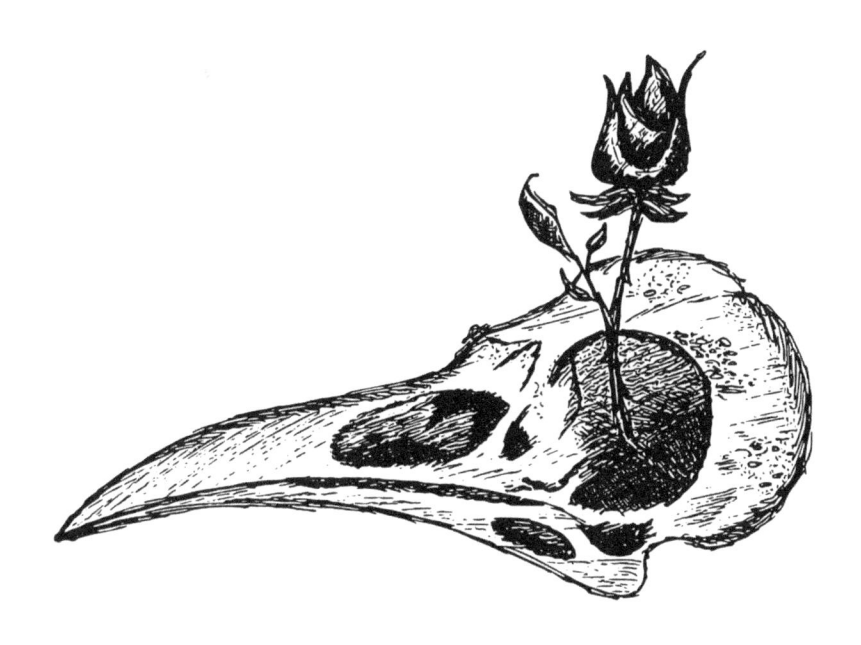

Seeing Sounds

Pastrano

thanks for listening

Seeing Sounds

Xavier Pastrano earned his BA in Creative Writing from Southeast Minnesota State University, his Masters of English from the University of North Dakota, and his Masters of Education in Teaching from the University of Sioux Falls. He currently resides in Sioux Falls with his wife and son where he teaches High School English and College Composition. When not teaching or writing, he enjoys reading, watching films, and playing in his band, Skin Of Our Teeth.

Pastrano

Acknowledgments:

This book wouldn't have been possible without Robert Swaney. Thank you for sharing your insight and knowledge as a writer and for your hard work in helping me bring this idea to life. Thank you, Janet Pischke, for your keen eyes and editing expertise. Lastly, thanks to the bands and artists that inspired this project; your art has moved me in ways I never thought possible, and I can only hope that mine does the same for others.

Listen to the playlist that inspired this book over at www.harsanpublishing.com/seeingsounds or by scanning the Spotify code below.

Seeing Sounds

CPSIA information can be obtained
at www.ICGtesting.com
Printed in the USA
LVHW061303300419
616094LV00003B/260/P